Message of the Day

Daily Spiritual Messages from Beyond the Veil

Facilitated by
Jeane R. Pothier

These channeled messages are given for entertainment purposes only.

ISBN: 978-0-615-25362-6

Acknowledgments

This book is dedicated to all of those dear ones who make the online version of these messages a part of their daily lives. I appreciate your support and above all, your emails to me of how these help you. This book is my way of bringing those messages into your hands. I especially thank Agnes Eeraerts for her encouragement along the way.

I am very grateful to those who have had a hand in the creation of these messages as they have evolved. Rosanne Dourado who had the idea of adding the **"If Today Is Your Birthday:"** section, and for Ray Goudie who did the programming for the website random selection of the Daily Message.

I also thank Kathy Nagel who told me long ago that I would actually have a website and people would come! You made a huge difference in my life and I am eternally grateful to have known you.

I'd like to thank Thorn who has been with me through this whole process and always encouraged me to reach for the highest and best.

Of course I have to thank those many angelic beings who showed up to allow me to share their words! I thank you for all that you do and for putting up with me.

I hope that this is simply the first of many volumes.

Hailey, Idaho

2008

Message of the Day Index

Message of the Day Index – continued

Give Your Body a Chance to Catch Up

I AM here this day, Raphael, the Angel of Healing and Transformation. I come to you this day at the behest of your own physical body, the physical expression of your divinity.

Over the last two months of your time you have been through tremendous shifts of energy. Your very being is now changed in ways that will slowly become manifest in your physical expression between now and the spring of the coming year. Perhaps at that time you might look back and not even recognize the person that is present this day.

Your body has been through these same tremendous shifts and frankly, it is tired. The physical body is the expression of your beingness, the outward expression of your Spirit. At this time it is asking something very simply and yet so very profound from you, something that if you choose to honor, will greatly facilitate all that is occurring on your physical plane at this time.

Your body would like some time to catch up! Yes! To catch up to the grand being who is driving the vehicle that is going through all the changes. Your body would like lots of water, lots of sleep, and dear one, a little more quiet time than you've been giving it lately.

Your body moves the energies that you perceive from all around you. Your body can at one time be your best friend and also your greatest enemy. You might feel at times that your body is holding you back from what you would like to achieve in your life, yet, this whole experience that you are allowing for yourself on this earth is all about the being going through this ascension process while embodied.

Dear one, allow your body to truly be your best friend. Give it time to catch up to you over the next few weeks. You will greatly need the support and allowance of your body before the end of this year and you will be grateful that you took the time now to take care of your body. For perhaps what you do not recognize quite so well as yet is that when you are taking care of your body you are taking care of yourself. You are putting out the message to all and asunder that you are worthy and that your body is an integral part of your process as a divine being having a human experience.

If you will listen, your dear body will tell you what foods it needs at this time to be fully supported in it's energy assimilation and movement. It will tell you what types of liquids it needs and when it needs more or less from you. The key thing here is to listen to the body when it talks to you. And it will talk in various languages that perhaps have not been so readily apparent to you in times previous.

Take a new look at pain, at discomfort, for these are indicators of energy that is not moving so well and so easily. Ask your body what the message in the pain or discomfort is for you. This can simply be an indicator of something that the body requires from you in the form of a different food, a different nutrient, more rest and so on.

It is time, way past time actually, to move into the divine relationship that you have been desiring to have with your body. And the more your dear body is aware that you are truly listening and responding to it's needs, the more it is ready to serve and support you in all ways possible. Do you need more strength and agility in order to have fun in your life? What does the body need from you in order to move into that place of experiencing these changes for you?

Give yourself time to sit and carry on a dialogue with your dear body and simply allow it to truly be the grand vessel that it is here on earth to be for you. It is truly up to you whether this dear body continues to be your greatest, trusted friend, or an enemy of aches and pains and difficulties you've set to overcome for yourself. The choice is always yours. We simply bring to you at this time the message that your body is more than ready to serve you and when you work in harmony with it, it too, is more easily able to move through these incredible, dynamic times in harmony with you.

I am delighted to be with you this day and I say in closing, Breathe!

If today is your birthday: This day comes to you but once a year and it is a time to celebrate yourself and all the ways that you are unique in this world. Do you value yourself my friend? Are you worth a grand party just for yourself in celebration of who you are?

I believe that you are!

I AM Raphael, Angel of Healing.

Take a Moment

I Am Raphael, the Angel of Healing and Transformation and I greet you this day with great joy! For you see, you have come to a place of being that is wondrous indeed, and a place that is worthy of recognition, if only for a brief moment along the journey that your soul is taking you.

This one much loved a television show called "Ally McBeal" and on that show there was a funny little man who used to "take a moment" and used this mannerism to great effect on those around him. They would indeed take a moment to stop and pay attention to what he was presenting to them.

And in this same way I too, am saying to take a moment and be with me in this energy, in this now and heed my words.

Many, many of you are feeling that you are in a place of nothingness, of missing something in your life, of not knowing where to go and what to do with yourself. And I am saying to you to celebrate this moment! Yes, celebrate where you are! Take a moment and celebrate that you are where you are!

For what this means is that you have completed all that you came to this earth to complete. You have learned the lessons, given yourselves the experiences, and now you are at a place of completion.

Yes, it feels strange and unnerving to you, for you are almost somewhat emptied out in your own energies. You have let go of so much that you feel as though there is nothing left of you! And yes, this too, is a good thing dear one!

For in this strange and hollow place that you find yourself, you now have the opportunity to bring in great wonders and great potentials for yourself. This is not a time of rushing off to take on another task, another job of serving another person, or even saving the world.

This is a time of recognizing that you have done an incredible job, that you have accomplished miracles! To recognize that now the worst of the worst is over for you and you can let down the barriers, let go of the struggles, and take a new look at your life.

Take a moment dear one, and look at what you truly desire for yourself in your life. Feel it, taste it, smell it. Walk into the dreams that have lain dormant in your heart of hearts. Walk into those early childhood fantasies of yourself and take another look at what you see there, for those dreams came from a pure and lovely place within you. They came from that place of knowing that nothing is impossible, that the world belongs to you and you can do anything.

Take a moment dear one, and be with you, breathing in the energies of completion, and give yourself the High Five's that are your due. For you have indeed accomplished the impossible, and if you can do that, then you can indeed, do anything!

I am delighted to be with you this day and I say in closing, Breathe!

If today is your birthday: Dear one, you are given a day once a year that is all about you and this is the perfect opportunity to take advantage of it! Take yourself to lunch or dinner, no one else, just you. Breathe with yourself and allow the love that is yours and yours alone to be given to you in gifting on this special day. Treat yourself well this day, for it is your own day of the year and being good and kind to yourself this day makes it even more special.

I AM Raphael, Angel of Healing and Transformation

Centeredness

It is I, Rafael, the Angel of Healing and Transformation who comes to sit with you this day. I have somewhat barged in to shift some energy and if you will breathe with me for this time we will begin.

There is an energy around you now that is contributing to feelings of doubt and anxiety. This energy is about trying to alter you from the course that you are determining for yourself. The doubts and anxieties that you are experiencing do not belong to you and with the breath you are easily and lovingly able to move them from you.

Therefore, we breathe with you this day with great love and joy for all that you are now allowing for yourself in your life. You have made choices that are the choices of a grand master and this will be so. Remember the energy of these choices and return to them when you feel the doubts and anxiety come to you.

Breathe my beloved, you are grand beyond imagining and all that you are desiring for yourself in your life is what you are now choosing to bring into fruition. Have no doubt and allow no one to tell you differently.

You are so dearly loved and all creation is here in support for you. I am delighted to be with you this day and I say in closing, Breathe!

If today is your birthday: Your birthday is not only a marking on the calendar of your birth date, it is also a bit of a milestone that you have come through another year. And with the energies as chaotic as they have been over this last year of time, that is no small matter! Breathe deep into your being this day and acknowledge that you are magnificent, for you truly are indeed!

I AM Raphael, Angel of Healing and Transformation

You Are Not Alone

We greet you this day dear one, with much joy.

We come in close in this safe and sacred space and we sit at your feet with much admiration and respect. Do you know that you are dearly loved by we who work with you on the other side of the veil? Do you know that there are legions of angels who eagerly await each request from you? Do you know that there are many, many angels who are here only to serve you? You are that beloved dear one. You are loved that much.

This is a time of much change and shifting of the energies in the world around you and within your very essence of who you are. At times it is like your own personal tsunami and at other times there is not so much shifting and you wonder what's happening that you see no changes in your life. We say to you beloved, that when you get an opportunity to "take a time out" then it is a safe and sacred space for you to breathe for a time and slow things down a bit.

We say to you that the energies around you are speeding up more and more every day. In this next period of time you will begin to feel this and will be able to appreciate those times when you can get off the road for a brief moment and catch your breath. Yet we know that you will also eagerly set foot once again back on that road, and with your eyes on the horizon, you will step forth with your head held high and your shoulders back, eagerly moving towards each new grand adventure that unfolds before you each day.

So this day beloved, we say to you that you are doing magnificently in your life, so matter how it may appear to you on the outside. The outer world does not so much reflect back to you what is happening with you on the other levels now. The more you step out of mass consciousness and the belief systems all around you, the less you will see this in your life. And the more this occurs the more we say to you to trust what you perceive inside of you.

Trust you, beloved. You are the truest barometer of your life. There is no one on this earth or anywhere else for that matter, who can decide for you what direction to take, what choices to make. It is time to trust the divine human that you are, for you are truly divine, and within you is all the knowledge and awareness, all the answers that you will possibly need at any time. It is time now to truly trust you and know that every decision, every choice that you make, is in divine service to you. Let go of the doubts and the hesitation and simply step into the reality that is you beloved, the divine human.

And you are so dearly loved!

If today is your birthday: We would love to be invited to the grand celebration of YOU! Yes, YOU! A party should be thrown in your honor because you are great and wonderful and you are making such an amazing and magnificent difference in your world. Take this day to acknowledge to yourself that you are worthy of great things and breathe in the energy that is here for you!

And There Is Love

I AM Sophia, the Goddess of the Divine Feminine and I am delighted to be here with you, in this moment, in this safe and sacred space. I come to you at this time to bring you an energy that is so very much taken for granted, abused so many times, and yet is so very much desired and needed by those on earth at this time.

Take a few deep breaths with me in this moment. You have been feeling so much sadness, so much grief as well. You have been wondering what your life is all about and how is it that nothing seems to be quite what you would like it to be.

You are nearing the completion of the transmutation of the old energies, the old patterns of behavior and the old ways of living and creating your life. You are feeling the ending of so many things in your life and this brings up the sadness. Because there is also the feeling that there are so many endings and where are the new beginnings?

Where are those dreams that you've been begging and pleading for in the middle of the night when you are feeling so lost and alone. Where are those changes in your life that you've been desiring to come to you for such a long time? Where is the divine love that you've been craving to have in your life?

Take another deep breath my dear one and simply be with me in this moment of time. This is a tiny moment of divine time, a time out of reality in many ways and it is yours in this moment for all time. For time is indeed all time, you simply see one fraction of this in your daily human existence and experience.

Take a deep breath and open yourself to the energies that are here for you this day. Open yourself to the remembrance of the Divine You and all that you are when you are not in physical form. Feel the love and the compassion that All That Is has for you, not only just in this moment, but always. Feel this, breathe this in, soak this into the very fiber of your being. Because this is where you're going my dear one.

You are moving into the embodiment of this energy in your human life! You are now moving into a new way of expressing yourself and in the many ways that you view your world around you. The worst of the worst is over, for all eternity, and you are now moving into the energy that has been waiting for millennium of time to come to you.

Breathe it in and know that it is yours, my dear one. Know that you have earned this moment in time unlike any other. It is yours to grasp and hold onto, it is yours to take into your very being. For you are the one who walked alone through the transformations of energies and you are the one who has emerged miraculously intact to come to this space!

And in this moment, this safe and sacred space my dear one, breathe in the love that is always yours. Breathe in the love that is your divine birthright. Breathe in the love that tells you that you are worthy beyond compare. Breathe in the love that is all around you.

I AM Sophia and it is a pleasure to be with you this day. Be well and know that all is well with your soul.

If today is your birthday: What you may not be aware of this day, is that all of Creation celebrates the day of your birth upon this earth. For you were birthed into a life that has not been easy and there has been much pain and heartache for you along the way. And on that special day that is uniquely yours each year, we all take a moment to give thanks that you choose to come here to make a difference for all of humanity. All who work with you and love you so very much are grateful that you are here.

You Are Stronger Than You Know

I AM Adamus, St. Germaine, and I step forward this day to share this time with you. Like so many, I have been waiting my turn to bring my energies through in this way. As always, it is pleasure to come closer and to sit with you and share this safe and sacred space in this moment.

You are experiencing a time now of constant shifts and shakes, things moving this way and that way and many ups and downs with those around you. Many whom you've despaired of every getting a clue to who you are or what your energies are all about are actually looking at you in a new way!

And still the world around feels strange and unsettling and you wonder how you will get through each day. How will you get through each moment as well!

Dear one, take this single moment, this single divine moment that is offered in this way, and take a few deep breaths. Take yourself off the treadmill of your life and step to the side. Step to the side and be at peace for this time. Breathe that peace deep into your being and take it fully into your physical body. For the human body needs the air right now, the divine Breath, more than at any other time.

In this moment my dear friend, feel the strength that is foundational with you come pouring back into you once more. Feel the courage that you have always had, the courage that has enabled you to walk this walk and to experience all that you have brought to yourself in your life. Feel this dear one and then see how very much you have accomplished as well!

You are not at the beginning of this journey dear one, you are far alone the way, striding along with your head held high and your steps firm and strong. You are not wavering, although at times you feel like your body might be unbalanced and shifting under you. Yet, dear one, in this moment of divine time, feel the core strength of who you truly are!

Feel this strength and remember what you've already been through in your life to get to this place! Those times are behind you, never to come again. Don't go looking for more of them, they will show up if you insist that you need to have them, but you have already made the choices necessary to be finished with those energies altogether. Now... you are simply going through the final phases of letting go of the old and allowing the new to come in.

So this day my dear one, allow yourself to remember that you are strong and can hold your head high with love and confidence in yourself, for you have already accomplished miracles by surviving!

I AM Adamus, St. Germaine and it is a delight for me to be here with you this day. I am always available and within reach. Simply ask for me to be with you and I am here. And so it is!

If today is your birthday: Dear one! You have survived another year in this ever changing consciousness! It's time to party and make much of this grand achievement and to acknowledge that you are magnificent beyond imaging for all that you bring to those around you by simply being here on earth at this time! Dance in the aisles with us this day! Raise your voice in song with us! Feel the energy of all who love you so very much coming together this day in celebration of YOU!

When You Feel Lost and Alone

I greet you this day my dear friend.

I AM your Soul Self and I love you dearly. I have stood by and watched as you traveled some tough roads, never faltering, never putting down the burdens that you've carried for eternities of time. You have kept a strength of purpose and mission that is unwavering in your life and it has served you well.

Yet dear one, I know that there have been those times when you thought that your heart would shatter into a million pieces because all you could see in your world were those who seemed to wish you ill. You wondered where your soul family was and why was it that you did not have a family that loved you and supported you in those ways that you truly needed to have.

You sat alone and you cried, frightened, weary of the hardships, wondering if things would ever change.

Yet deep within your soul essence of who you are on this earth, there continued to burn a small flame of knowing that would somehow flare up when you most needed it to appear for you.

Somehow you were able to stoke this flame of knowing your divine self, knowing of me, and it kept you going in your life.

In the darkest regions of your human self you held to the knowing that there was a reason that you were here on the earth and it wasn't to be who your parents believed you should be. It wasn't to act like others believed you should act.

It wasn't to say what was expected of you and it certainly wasn't to live a life like everyone else around you. You were different from the very beginning and this has been, in the same moment, a cause of pain and a banner of joy.

You knew that you were here for some undefined reason that was escaping you most of the time. Yet there were those small moments out of time when you could feel that you were here to make a difference in some way. Even if that meant that you took on great hardships, great pain and even greater misunderstandings of yourself from those around you.

And now, more than ever, you are feeling your divine self coming back to share this life with you now. It is as though all the tears, all the heartache and disappointments have been worth it somehow. For now, more than at any other time, you are coming to see who you truly are and this person is a really terrific person!

Breathe in the energies that are here for you this day. Breathe in the knowing that no matter what has come before this time, each day now is different, brighter and far more clear for you. For you are now in harmony with ME, your Soul Self, and together we are changing your life for the better in all ways.

When you are feeling lost and alone, reach for ME and I am here. Call me to you in any moment and I AM here with you. We are now becoming one and with this blending, this joining, comes a greater ease of living, a greater confidence and most of all, a greater integrity in expression who you truly are in your life.

For when you are blended, united and integrated with ME, your Soul Self, there is no one with greater authority for you in your life than YOU! You are the grand determiner of what your life will be and how it unfolds for you, for this we are creating together at a level of mastery unavailable to the majority of humans.

And my dear one, you have earned this through your blood, your tears, your heartache, and above all, through your courage to keep going when it would have been so easy to lay down and simply die.

I AM here for you now and always and together there is a grand life waiting to be explored together!

I am delighted to be with you this day and I say to you in closing, Breathe!

If today is your birthday: With this day you have come to a time of closure with an old life. Take a deep breath and give yourself permission to step out of that old life, which fits you now like a suit of clothes that hangs on you without shape or fit. Give yourself permission to hold your head high this day and look around at what is here for you now. Give yourself permission to allow this day to be one of new beginnings for you, a time of awakening and of sharing with those who love you so very much, as we gather together here to celebrate the grandness of YOU!

In This Moment

I AM Raphael, the Angel of Healing and Transformation and it is a great pleasure to step forth and appear to you this day, even if it is only in the form of words upon a page with an energy chaser, so to speak.

I am glad to come forth, for it gives me an opportunity to interact in ways that I have not had much opportunity to do in the human existence over the last 2,000 years. Oh yes, I've been written about and there's been talk all over the Universe, but this is personal now, this is just between you and I and this is a great delight for me to share.

Take a deep breath my friend. Take a deep breath and step over an invisible doorstep and come into my space as I have come into yours. Come into a space that you are actually very familiar with when you are not in physical form on the earth.

In this space there is great wonder, as all humans who have ever dreamed of heaven have brought those creations here and made them manifest. There is magic and there is love and there is above all, a great light.

In this moment my friend, you are a grand part of that light, even though you are still in physical form on the earth. You have a part of yourself, a part of your Soul Self, that remains here, for you are divine and are many things at the same time. You always leave a part of yourself here that is a bit of a placeholder for you so that you can be sure that you will find yourself once again in this place, in this moment.

The light that you are in the physical form on the earth right now, in this moment, is reflected where others wait for you, on this side of the veil. At any time one may come and view that light and know how you are doing, what you are doing, and how your life is progressing for you.

In this moment, your light shines brighter than ever before and it can be somewhat startling at times. For in the toughest of times, in the darkest of moments, it flares up and blazes brighter than the brightest sun!

Feel this my friend. Feel the light that is the essence of you. And in this moment, know that you are so much more than you ever believe yourself to be, even on the lightest of days in your physical form. For you are a Human Angel and stood in line to come to earth and to make a difference by your very presence. And your very presence there on the earth now, is what is bringing light to all of the Universe.

I AM Raphael and I am delighted to share this moment with you. Be well and know that all is well with your soul. You are doing magnificently and I love you so very much.

If today is your birthday: Today is special because it is the marking of the day that you made it here to earth! You actually survived the process of selection and choices and the transition from spirit to human. You have survived and we all celebrate the life that is you. Take this moment and receive the love that is here for you now, in celebration of who you are and the difference that you make in this world.

Listen to Your Self

I AM Adamus, St. Germaine.

It is a privilege and a delight to be here with you this day, in this moment. I watch over all that you are choosing in your life and I am in awe of all that you are allowing for yourself now, in these New Energies.

I see those times when you stumble though. I see those times when you are so sure that you are doing the wrong thing, taking the wrong direction in your life and that nothing good will come to you. I see how these thoughts, feelings and emotions affect you and it brings sadness to my heart.

For dear one, dear friend, you are doing magnificently! Hear my words! Feel the energy that I bring to you this day in this moment! Feel the love and the compassion that is here for you and know, deep in your heart of hearts, that all is well with your soul.

As the waves of energies continue to bombard the earth during this period of time, you will be experiencing much energy that is actually on its way out of your life. You will be experiencing old situations, old relationships, old lives coming to you that you felt were long completed and here they are, just like you've never left them behind.

So what do you do my dear friend, when this happens to you?

Take a moment, like this very moment, and stop what you're doing altogether. Stop and be still. Breathe deeply, and ask for the quiet, the peace and the knowing that comes from your own Soul Self to be present for you. Move into those energies and listen my friend, listen to what comes to you in that moment.

Your Soul Self has all the answers that you could ever possibly need to have in that moment. You can ask anything and the energy will answer to you, for you are the Master on earth and all is here to support and to serve you.

Listen to your Soul Self. Listen to the energies that tell you that all is well. Listen to the voices of your own group and runners who are here for you, always. Listen to the inner knowing that you have, that is your Divine Birthright, which says that you are more than ok, that you are indeed, magnificent! And in that moment of listening my friend... let go of everything around you that tries to tell you differently, for it doesn't belong to you and it is time to release it out of your life.

I AM Adamus, St. Germaine and it is a delight to share this moment with you. Trust yourself, love yourself and know that all is indeed well with your soul.

If today is your birthday: You are blessed this day with that very special energy that comes to you from all who serve you on this special day. It is a gift to you from All That Is and it comes to you in the deepest appreciation for you and you alone. You are deeply loved and blessed for having the courage to be here on the earth at this time, to do what you are doing, and to be making the difference that you are making with all who come to pass your way. We are grateful to you.

How Can I Help in This World?

I AM Zadkiel, an Archangelic Angel of the higher realms.

I step forth this day to be here with you at this time. I ask that for a moment you simply allow yourself to be quiet and to breathe in the energies that are now present for you in this format, for it takes a bit of adjusting as you read these words. Much energy is being delivered to you and much is available for your potentials in your life.

I come to you this day because you are at a bit of an impasse in your own life... wondering what comes next and wondering as well, are you on the right path for yourself. I come to you this day because I am one who watches over human angels and am always available to you, to walk with you and to carry on a conversation at your own leisure. There is no magic involved in our communication... it simply is.

There are essentially two ways that a divine human, an aware and conscious human can "help" during these momentous times. And I say to you at this time that in your heart of hearts... you already know what these are for you. For you are one who has followed your own guidance quite well for many years and has had occasional doubt and unsurety in your life that you have worked your way through to find a clarity of resolution that serves you. I applaud your strength and courage and I applaud that you choose to walk to the beat of a different drummer in your life. This serves you well my friend.

The greatest way that one divine human can help another is to be authentic in your own life, in your own expression. Too many times a human will do whatever it takes to fit in somewhere, to follow the crowd and to act like another so as to not stand out, for fear of reprisal or judgment or even condemnation. This has served you well at times while at others it has brought great heartache as well as you have felt hidden and unseen.

For you know that you are not quite like everyone else and in that knowing you have no desire to try to fit into the ways of others.

This following of the crowd mentality is changing my friend, and you are one who is somewhat stepping outside the box of the old characteristics so as to bring new energy and new ideas into an old energy foundation. Be at peace with this my friend, for you are being well supported and well guided in your endeavors. Trust that you are being given all that you will need in any given moment and that all is well for you.

The second greatest attribute that a divine human can express that is of assistance to all in this world, is to follow your dreams, and that is in spite of what is told to you, what is held to be the common belief and what is constantly being expressed to you from others. Your dreams come directly from your own soul source and are the way that the divine soul essence comes to you and speaks of it's desires and reminders of what you had set up for yourself before you came into this human experience.

When you follow your dreams you are essentially saying to others, allowing others to see for themselves, that there is more to this life than what appears on the surface in all ways. When you allow yourself to live those dreams you are saying to another that it is possible to be of such value and to matter so much to oneself that it is quite permissible to have those dreams, to have a great life that comes from being true to yourself!

For this life, this expression the divine human in physicality, is about remembering how divine the spirit is, and the spirit is connected to the human physicality. So many humans have forgotten their divine birthright and now live lives of quiet desperation that lead to depression, suicide, rage and deep anger, expressed outwardly in the world.

When one is living their dreams, allowing themselves to be at peace with who they are and being grounded and centered in those knowings, then there is a peace and tranquility that is expressed outwardly to all they come into contact with in their lives. This is what changes the world my friend.

So my friend, I say to you this day that the best way you can help is to be who you truly are and to **trust** that which YOU are. You are not who you are in this life by mere accident! This is what was chosen by you and your own council of angels long before you came to this human experience!

Breathe in the energy of this in this moment. Feel the love that your own Soul Source has for you and know that you are very loved by All That Is. Follow your dreams and be at peace with where your life takes you. For when the divine master lives a life that is a pure expression of who they are then others are able to see this for themselves and will take much hope from this, and perhaps even give themselves permission to step into and live their own dreams.

I AM Zadkiel and I am delighted to share this time with you. Be open to the divine guidance that you receive, doubt not that you are hearing from your own soul source with the greatest of love and compassion for you. Live your life from that place of your own divinity and know that all is well with your soul.

If today is your birthday: This day is the day that belongs to you. It is yours to do with as you choose. It is a day to love yourself and to bless yourself for all that you have experienced in this human life. Take a moment and love yourself my friend. Give thanks and many blessings to yourself for being here during this time, for allowing yourself to be who is here to make a difference. You are beloved beyond imagining!

Beyond the Veil

I AM Xandra, one of the infinite number of angelic beings who are on the other side of the veil. I AM one of the many who are now able to come forth and share these energies with you now and it is of this that I wish to speak about this day.

I greet you with great jubilation and delight, for it has long been anticipated that the veils would one day thin and those of us who assist so diligently on this side of the veil would one day be able to come close to sit with you once more.

For when you are on our side of the veil we are great friends as are you with many, many beings on this side. We all share the energies of All That Is as One. And in that ONEness energy we know one another with a great intimacy that is not possible on the earthly plane.

Yet, my dear, dear friend, that is not what I came forth to speak to you about this day. Instead, let me sit with you for just a moment and breathe with you, for in the breath lies the magic of that time of being Home, of being once again part of All That Is. Feel the energies that are present with you this day, for there are indeed a great many who sit here with you in this moment.

With recent shiftings in the energetic patterns of all humanity as well as the earth herself, the veils are now thinner than ever. It is this that now enables your own angels, group and runners, to be more present for you in a more conscious way. They are all eager to be put to use in new ways, to assist you as they have always done on this side of the veil.

Yet, they are now available to you in ways that have never before been anticipated and these ways are here for you to explore and to decide for yourself. How will you use and play with those divine beings who are now closer than ever to you? What will you talk about and what will it feel like for you to remember that friendship, that unity of thought and being that is the energy of Home for you?

The greatest gift that comes with the thinning of the veils is that you can know, in any moment, with every breath, truly know that you are not alone on your journey, in your explorations. You have friends beyond number and they all love you and desire only the highest and best for you in your awakening. They are here for you in ways that you will come to know as your days unfold in your life.

And in this divine moment as this information is being brought to you, I simply ask that you take this moment and breathe in the grand and glorious love that is here for you, the divine human. Feel the closeness to All That Is that is your divine birthright. Feel the infinite number of angels who sit by your side and simply love you without agenda or expectation. Feel this my dear friend, and know that there is much more where this love comes from and it's all for you.

I AM Xandra and I am deeply grateful for this moment of being able to come forth and sit with you this day. Welcome me in and I am here for you at any time. Breathe in the love and breathe in the closeness of family that is now more available to you than at any time in all of Creation!

If today is your birthday: Today you are blessed beyond all other days, for on this day we who sit with you and share your energies celebrate the coming into the physical sharing that is done with your own divine being. For it is while in the physical form that the most magic happens in the expression of the divine being. And this life is coveted by many who are waiting their own turn to be here. Enjoy this day and breathe in all the acclaim and celebration that is happening on this side of the veil. You are truly never alone!

Sometimes You Just Need a Hug

I AM Sophia, Goddess of the Divine Feminine. I have worked through the eons with the Mary energies, the Magdalene energies and I have been a supporting energy for all those who choose to live in their heart energies and to express their heart energies to others.

I walked with the Knights Templar as they sought to integrate their own masculine energies with the Divine Feminine so as to find balance and unity. I wept with deep grief when I saw how those endeavors came to an end, much as such movements with others have ended, with the masculine energies not being able to find harmony and balance with the divine feminine.

And now you are seeking to do much the same with your own life; to find balance and unity with your own energies. There is much in your outer world that does not like this and there is much energy that is seeking to try to dissuade you from choices such as these.

Yet my friend, you are living in authenticity with your own higher being, your own soul source, and you know that this is what is your own highest and best. I am here this day to support your choices as you move towards sovereignty and unity. I support you, along with legions of angels now on the other side of the veil. I am here with you this day to bring you a small moment out of time as you move through your own life in it's human expression.

I ask that in this moment, this time of being in a safe and sacred space, that you allow yourself to receive a galactic hug as it were, from all who are here for you now. Can you do this my friend? Can you give yourself permission to take a deep breath and allow those energies of divine love and compassion to come into your own physical being and be received by every cell of your body?

This love, this divine hug, is just for you now. There is no one else here in this receiving, only you. All of this energy is focused just for you and it is yours alone and you need not turn and share it with another. Take this energy deep within your own heart and know that you are so dearly loved, that you are supported in so many ways as you struggle to live the best life that you can.

Yes, I know that there are those days when you wonder what you're doing here and how to keep going, and I say to you that you are not alone in those feelings. They have been integral even in the hearts of the Great Ones, of the Marys' who struggled with their own divinity in long ago times.

Be at peace my dear friend, and know that you are doing magnificently! Take this divine hug that is yours today and be at peace with yourself. For you are grand indeed and so worthy of an infinite numbers of such hugs... all just for you.

If today is your birthday: Receive this day the infinite blessings of all who are here for you with the greatest of love and admiration. You walk this earth with so much hidden from yourself, yet you get up each day and continue on your journey. You are loved beyond imagining and All That Is supports your every choice. Rejoice this day, for we do, that you are here on earth at this time, making a difference in the human consciousness.

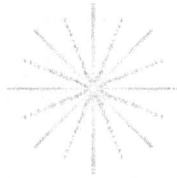

The Thanks Flow Both Ways

I AM Tobias, of the *Crimson Council, and so it is that I come to you this day to add my voice to that of the multitude of voices that desire to speak with you this day.

So many times we sit with you in those times in your life when you are feeling less than the divine angels that you truly are. We, all those who love you and are always available for you on this side of the veil, at times even weep with you when you are feeling so sad and lonely.

And then you will suddenly make a big shift of energy, a gigantic leap of consciousness, and you will then come to us and express your great thanks for the support and love that you have received during those times of depression and deep grief and sadness.

I am here this day my friend, along with a multitude of angels who love you so very much, so express my personal thanks to you. I also speak with the voice of the compilation of energies from all your personal energies as I express these energies to you in this moment.

The thanks and appreciation flows both ways, my friend. For when you are thanking those who love you so very much and share their own energies with you during the times of difficulty and uncertainty, they are in turn thank you for all that you are doing to make a difference in this life.

I ask that in this moment that you take yourself apart from your busy world and breathe with all of us for a moment. Breathe deeply of the deep and infinite gratitude that is here this day. Breathe deeply of the appreciation that we all have for you in every moment of your earthly expression. Breathe deeply of this love and gratitude and know that without you doing what you have been doing, there would be less love and light in this world.

I AM Tobias of the Crimson Council and I add my personal gratitude to you this day for all that you are allowing for yourself, the grand and glorious steps that you are taking in every moment. Even when you are stepping out in trepidation and fear of the unknown, you are still stepping out with courage and grace. You are making a difference in this world in every moment and with each breath that you are taking.

Now take this moment and breathe in the gratitude that is here for you in great abundance and honor yourself as we honor you.

If today is your birthday: Blessed be you the divine human who walks the earth this day, living your life as best you can, without a manual telling you how everything works or should work! You are lighting the way and you are shining the light of your own divinity for all to see. Celebrate this day as we celebrate you!

* - For more information about the Crimson Council visit the website: www.crimsoncircle.com

And When It's Time to Move On

And so it is dear one, that I, Tobias of the Crimson Council, come forward to share this time with you.

It is a grand time in your life, even though it may not appear to be so at this very moment.

Yet it is a grand time and there is much more to come for you! There are potentials that are appearing daily for you in areas that you have only had glimpses of up until now. There is a gradual unfolding that will be taking place and each day will be bringing you a tiny hint of what's coming to you.

Yet what I come to you this day to speak about is not the future but is the present and your own personal life. For in the vast changes that you have been bringing to yourself you are now seeing that your outer world is less and less compatible with the divine being that you are allowing yourself to be.

How do you deal with those in your life who are uncomfortable with the vast unfolding of your own divinity? How do you talk to those who have no desire to see you change and perhaps are fighting you in ways that are increasingly uncomfortable for you?

There is nothing that you can do for those who desire to keep you in an old place, as they are divine ones on their own spiritual journey, and are God also. It is not your job here in this incarnation to change the heart or mind of another and any attempts to do so will only bring about that "beating your head against a brick wall" kind of feeling within yourself.

There are times my dear friend, when you reach a place where you can no longer be around people who do not support you in the ways that you deserve to be supported. Perhaps it's a spouse who is used to an old energy dynamic and doesn't wish to make any changes.

Perhaps it's a child who is so used to having their own way that when their parental support is changing they rant and rave and throw tantrums because they fear anything new.

There are times my dear friend, when the greatest thing that you can do for yourself is to simply give yourself permission to let go of those old relationships and move on. For many times, more often than you might believe, it is you who is the one holding on! And when you simply open your hand and let it go energetically, then it can leave you and move on to it's own resolution.

So this message this day is about honoring yourself in those times when you know you can move on and truly desire to move on and yet have been not quite ready to allow this for yourself. Now is the time my friend to open your hand and release your grasp of those old relationships that do not serve you and do not support the divine being that you are.

Give yourself permission to have those ones in your life who honor you and cherish you, who are delighted to share you life with you and only have the wish to support you in your own endeavors rather than to feed on your higher vibrational energies. You deserve to have such ones in your life, those who respect you and desire only the best for you. And these new relationships come as you release the old ones my friend. And so this day, can you give yourself permission to move on?

I AM Tobias and it is a pleasure to be here with you this day. I honor all that you are doing in your life and I have greatly enjoyed my time with you.

I am delighted to be with you this day and I say in closing, Breathe! And so it is.

If today is your birthday: What better day than today to make a grand change in your life that serves you! What better gift this day than to make a choice that says to All That Is that you do matter, that you are of value and you deserve to be treated with the greatest of care and respect! Give this gift to yourself this day!

A Time to be Still

I AM the Archangel Raphael and it is an honor to be here this day with you, to sit with you once more and to share my energies with you.

There is much that is happening in your life and much that you have allowed yourself to release and in this moment you are feeling an emptiness of spirit, an emptiness of that which you have long known as your own energies. It is a delight for me to once more be here with you and to share this time.

In the world as it is now, during these momentous times, it is easier and easier to become so busy, so hurry scurry, that there is less and less time for you, yourself. There is less time to have those moments of peace and stillness and less time to find your own place of centeredness.

This can be quite damaging to you as you long for those times of inner peace and tranquility and feel that they should always be present for you, and why indeed, are they not? What is it that you are not doing right or correctly that would allow you to be perfectly at peace in all moments of your life?

You live in momentous times and this is what you have chosen for yourself my friend. You have chosen to be of this world, not out of this world! And as one who is of this world, you are subject to all the energies that are constantly swirling around you, interacting with your own energies and dancing, dancing, dancing with it all.

This is not a life of retreat and continuous introspection. This is not a life where you are able to take yourself away from everything and everyone around you. This is a life that you have chosen to share your energies with others and to experience what it is like to be of a certain vibration while those around you are not.

This is a life that was purposely set up to be one of near constant interaction and diversion, yet my friend, it is also a life where you have the choice of how much you interact with others. You have the choice to take yourself away and to take care of your own inner needs and with this I say to you, that when you take yourself away from the energies of others, you are truly serving you.

You are serving you in that you are saying to All That Is that your inner world, your inner peace, are more important than making sure another being is receiving your energies. That is not your job my friend, you are not here to serve another. You are here to make a difference in this world because you are bringing yourself experiences that other human beings have never had before. You are not here to take care of another, you are here to integrate all that YOU are and in that integration and merging with your own soul, to then be the greatest expression that you can be.

It's ok to be still my friend, to take yourself away from the energies of others and to be with you. It's ok my friend to know that there are those times when the energies of others are more damaging and non-serving to you that they could be. It's ok my friend to take yourself apart and be at peace with you, for when you do this, you are recognizing and acknowledging to you, the grand being, that you know what serves you most.

There is nothing outside of you that is better for you, more healthy for you, more beautiful for you, than you yourself. You find this divine being when you allow yourself to be quiet and to be still. This is where you find that inner core that is truly YOU and this is when you give yourself that breather, that time out that is much like a wind beneath your wings when you fly in the outer world. It's ok my friend to be still, to take time for you, as much time as you need, for this is the foundation of being at peace with the outer world.

I AM Raphael and it is a gift for me to be here with you this day. Give yourself the same type of gift by being still with yourself. There is truly no finer gift than that connection with yourself my friend. Gift yourself each day and see how much more at ease you become with your outer world.

If today is your birthday: This is a grand day to be with you and also to share your energies with others. Begin with the time with you, sitting quietly and allowing the love that your soul has for you to be present for you. Receive the love that is here for you and know that you are loved beyond imagining!

You Have All the Time You Need

I am here dear one, I AM Raphael, the Angel of Healing and Transformation and I come close to sit with you now, in this safe and sacred space of energy.

Your world has gotten increasingly busy and hectic and you are finding that your own energies are being stretched and pulled and shaken every which way. And I say to you that this will increase over the next few years of time. And so my friend, in this space, I ask that you take this moment to sit and breathe with me now. Take a moment out of that hectic, crazy day and sit with me and be at peace in this energy.

All around you are the illusions of created deadlines and schedules. I refer to these as created illusions because on another level of existence and energy, they are not at all "real" in the sense of being something that has great impact on your life. These are created as a form of control by others and you only agree to conform to these because it is how the game of life is played.

When you step out of mass consciousness these types of restrictions and boundaries have less and less impact upon you in your physical realm. Oh, there is still the structure of a 24-hour day and your attempts to fill as much of that time with what you perceive to be meaningful activities, yet that too, is an illusion.

For my friend, when you are fully present in the moment, in the expansive NOW that is your true reality on this plane of existence, there is more than enough time! There is more than enough time for you complete all the tasks that you set for yourself each day. There is more than enough time for you to have moments to be quiet with yourself and to breathe.

And my friend, there is more than enough time for you to have the life that you desire to have and experience. You feel so many times that you are running out of time, that your life is speeding out of control and you will never arrive at the various goals that you have set for yourself.

And all around you, you can perceive that everyone else is feeling a bit of this constraint of not having enough time.

And I say to you this day my friend, when you are feeling just the opposite, that there is never enough time for you, then pinch yourself or do something else in this moment to bring yourself out of the energy of mass consciousness. For when you have the perception that there is never enough time for you to do all that you desire to do, then you are simply stuck deep in mass consciousness and it's "time" to pull yourself out of it!

My friend, you have all the time that you need in any given moment. For in the now, all time is infinite, and that is the reason that all dreams, all visions, all goals and desires are possible when created in the now moment. Let go of the worry of not having enough time and step into the soul knowing that you do indeed, have all the time that you need in any moment.

I AM Raphael and it is a pleasure to sit with you this day and share my energies with you. You are so dearly loved! Remember to breathe!

If today is your birthday: Today above all days is a day to take lots and lots of time to celebrate you, the divine being. For your day of birthing is one to celebrate, for this world would not be the same were you not here my friend. Enjoy!

When There Is Loss

I Am here this day my friend. I AM Raphael, Angel of Healing and Transformation and I come forward this day to speak about the loss of loved ones, the letting go of those who share your life in the physical and above all, the grief and emptiness that accompanies their passing.

Because the human consciousness does not remember what it's like to leave the physical body and move into the other realms, there is the generalized belief that death is a harsh thing, that it's painful in some way and greatly frightening for the being who is leaving.

This is not the case my friend. The spirit that leaves the physical body is gone in an instant and there is no pain in the passing. There is a moment of betweeness during the transition and then there is actually a great relief as the density of the physical body connection is severed.

There is a feeling of joy as the spirit leaves the physical body, for the true nature of spirit is lightness and ease of movement and it is only when the spirit is attached to a physical body that the energies are slowed down and fully experienced in a manner that many could describe as being too much, or even overkill in a way.

When someone you care about very much leaves this earth, there is great joy on this side, for there are many who await the passing of those who have served out their time on the earth. There are grand celebrations and there is much joy in reunions between souls who have long been parted from each other. There is no sadness in this transition and it brings us sadness when we see how humans respond to the passing of someone close to them.

When it is a dear pet companion the grief is somewhat different, for there is more a feeling that there will never come another time of reunion of souls as it were. I come to you this day to tell you that this is not the case and in this moment I ask that you breathe in the reassurance that I bring to you that those who leave the physical will always be reunited in the other realms, for such is the nature of Oneness, that all are One.

And while you may feel the great loss and emptiness of one who has left you, they are not truly gone from your existence. Their energies exist on another realm and they are at times very close to you indeed. There will be those moments when you sit quietly and allow yourself to release control and belief systems and then, in that precious moment, you will feel their energy sitting close to you. For there is such love that exists on this side of the veil and it is so much easier to flow that love without the density of the physical body!

The spirit of those who pass on will never die, for the soul is eternal. This is also the case for those dearly loved pet companions who's life span is some much shorter than humans would like it to be. Those dear pet companions stay close and many times will be dancing around the feet of the one who they once shared much time and companionship with on earth. Their love continues and they are amongst the first who stand in line to greet you when you yourself make the transition from this earth.

Take heart my friend, for all is never lost completely. And while there is nothing that can truly take away the grief and loss that you are feeling, hold close to the knowing that one day you will see each other again and there will be much joy and gladness in that reunion!

And in this moment my friend, feel the love and compassion from all of us who work so closely with you and hold you close. We feel your heartache and cry tears of sadness with you as you go through what you are now experiencing. You are not alone in this and even when you feel that you are now facing a time of aloneness, you will always be surrounded by more angels than you can possibly imagine.

Give yourself the opportunity to grieve, for it is a divine human attribute and it serves you well to experience this and the knowing that it is also indicative that you cared deeply and will miss your loved one. There is much honor in this and do not for a moment deny yourself this releasing of emotions with the feelings, for they serve you much. You are a divine human and this is a human experience.

I AM Raphael and I am here with you my friend. Know that you are dearly loved and that one day, all will be understood and you will once more stand with all those whom have shared your life and your love in this human experience. This transition now is just a moment out of time.

Breathe, my friend, and allow yourself to flow into your emotions. They honor who you are in every moment.

If today is your birthday: You are so very loved and honored in all ways. It is the day of your birth when we celebrate just a bit more, send you just a bit more love and compassion, for it is a grand day indeed that you chose to be birthed upon this earth, to do a job that takes much courage and strength of purpose. You are loved beyond imagining!

Boundaries

I AM Adamus, St. Germaine and it is a pleasure for me to be here with you this day. There is so very much going on in the world around you and it is good when you take a moment to stop and allow yourself to breathe and be still.

This day I desire to speak about boundaries. This is a word that has many definitions and can be seen one way in a particular situation and then take on a whole new meaning for another situation. What I share with you this day is regarding boundaries between oneself and those who are now awakening and looking around and suddenly seeing someone that they believe will or might rescue them from the path that they have currently been traveling in their life.

What I am saying with this is that more and more people are coming awake as it were, to a whole new world around them. There is a massive shifting of consciousness and many people are looking around and asking themselves what else is there in their lives. They are asking what purpose they have in their lives and how can they live a better life.

Many times these ones have come to the end of a painful and harsh road of trauma and drama and have had enough of those to such an extent that they are now looking for an escape of some kind. And in far too many cases, they are looking for someone or something outside of themselves to "fix them" or to come to their rescue with answers as to what they should do now in their lives.

Take a moment and breathe with me now, for you are feeling an energy that has been slowly encroaching upon you and you have been increasingly uncomfortable with this for yourself. You did not go through all that you have experienced in your life so that you could rescue another.

Yes, you could teach another what you have learned. You could share your own story and experiences with another and this would be an appropriate expression of your divine beingness.

What does not serve you and does not honor you my friend, is to be placed in a position where another is giving you their power, is asking you to tell them what to do and them expecting you to rescue them from a life that they have had great fun and experience creating!

Feel this my friend and breathe with me. You are not here to rescue another nor to fix another and if you find yourself caught up in situations where another is attempting to place this energy upon you, then it is time to firm up your personal boundaries and be strong.

In a world that is becoming more and more chaotic as the old energies leave and others are breaking down before the ingrowth of new energies, there is more energy of fear, of disillusion, of discontent and the anxiety associated with old systems leaving and nothing as yet coming to take a new place.

Within this shifting are many who are looking outward for a lifeline and you may be finding yourself pulled and grabbed onto by those around you. And yes, there are times when you might find this to be a gratifying experience as others come to have a greater appreciation for what you do have to share.

Yet my friend, sovereignty does not mean taking on the problems of another person. It does not mean fixing another or taking on their energies as your own. You have walked in the shoes of a master long enough to know that you help no one when you try to shoulder what they have chosen to experience for themselves.

Boundaries are about standing in your own power and simply sharing an energy with another that they too, can remember that they have all the answers that they need in any given moment.

Boundaries for yourself are about not allowing another person to use you or exploit you from their own place of fear. Boundaries are about the firmness of your own power and stance when it comes to those clients that may be calling you in the middle of the night because they want you to tell them what to do when they feel fear.

Take time each day my friend, to reaffirm your own boundaries and to stand strong in your place in your life. Remember that you are the teacher and not the bearer of the burdens of others. You do no one any good when you take on their energies as though they are your own to clear and release. You do no one any good when you take on their karma when you have completed your own a long time ago. You do no one any good when you get lost in the trauma and drama of another and most of all, you dishonor yourself when you act in the role of being the savior of another. There was only one savior in the world and that is not your role.

Be strong my friend and be at peace with refusing to take the power from another. When you help another to be strong in their own knowing you are far more beneficial in this than in anything else. Allow no one to give away their power to you and stand strong in your own knowing that you owe no other being your energy or your life.

I AM Adamus St. Germaine and it is a delight to be here with you this day. Remember my words, for you will find that you are tossed and turned during the times ahead and many may come to your door to cling to you as to a lifeline. When you take on the energies of another, regardless of the loving desire to be of help, you are in effect on the way to drowning yourself. Feel this my friend and stay strong in the knowing of who you are and that a Master teaches, they do not perform the lessons and experiences for their students.

I AM with you this day and I say in closing... Breathe!

If today is your birthday: You are so greatly honored this day and all days. The day of the birthing of your physical being is a day of empowerment for this commemorates your choice to come here during this time to help make a difference. And make a difference in this world is exactly what you are doing! You are dearly loved and greatly supported and you are never alone.

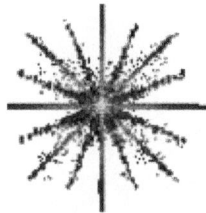

Begin Anew

Greetings Dear One!

I AM Raphael, the Angel of Healing and Transformation, and I dearly love to come sit with you in this manner, sharing my energies with yours. I love to have this time out with you, when you allow yourself to be quiet and at peace with your world for this moment, and to allow the energies available to you in this medium to come to you.

Find that inner peace is not always so easy lately. There is so much to-ing and fro-ing of outer forces all around you, setting up whirlpools of divergent energies that can cause anxiety, tension, even bring up old fears and doubts. So very much of this energy is coming from those around you who do not trust themselves and therefore, do not trust the world that they see before them. They have learned, unconsciously, to believe that they have no control over what happens to them and this is not an easy world to live in at times.

With all these divergent energies swirling around it makes it more difficult for the divine human to sort through and weed out the energies that truly serve you. You wonder about the dreams and ambitions that you have and if these are possible for you, if you are making the right choices and even if you are serving yourself and the world by your very life.

During especially chaotic times the energies can shift under your feet and around you in the blink of an eye. You can make a choice to go in a particular direction and then in the next blink find that you are being led in an entirely different direction. How confusing this can be! And in each change and shift you find yourself wondering once again, what is your best option, what is the best direction for you, what is the best choice to make in this moment.

What the divine human struggles with more than anything is the leaving behind of the old choices and their inherent energies and easily moving into the energies of the new choice. More often than not you will revisit the old choices and try to make sure that you aren't leaving behind something that you might need at a later time!

What I bring to you this day, in this moment dear one, dear friend, is the knowing that in each moment, with each new choice that you are making, you can begin anew. You can wipe the slate clean of any previous choices, let them all go, and be stepping fully into the new choices without worrying that you've left something valuable behind you.

Begin anew in each moment that you desire to have a new choice, make a new dream and follow a new path. Begin anew and know that your very soul will bring to you anything that you could possibly need from previous experiences and you need not worry about leaving anything valuable behind.

Begin anew and begin with an ease of heart and spirit. Begin anew without old baggage and behaviors and as you do begin anew, simply know that in every moment you can again make a new choice. For the divine human knows that nothing is "written in stone" and change is the nature of this existence during these interesting times. And with each new choice, each new beginning, you are fully supported by all who love you so much and work with you on this side of the veil.

I AM Raphael and it is a pleasure to be here with you this day. Let go of any energies that don't belong to you and be the divine human that you came here to this earth to be. Breathe in this energy of renewal and know that all is well with your soul.

If today is your birthday: Today is an especially good day to begin anew. Celebrate all that you've known thus far, bless it and express your gratitude and then let it go. There is more waiting to come to you and with each breath you invite in the new to be here for you. You are so dearly loved!

To Find What Is Yours

I greet you this day dear one! I AM Zaihada of the Sirian League of Light and it is a pleasure and delight to be here with you at this time and all times. I do not so much need to experience time for myself, yet it is always interesting to come to sit with those who read this and be in the energy where they are in that moment.

There is great confusion around you now. You have come to a bit of a crossroads of sorts and are standing there, scratching your head, looking first up one road and then down another. What choice should you make in this moment? What is the right choice? What is the choice that you make is the wrong choice for you and it hurts you, brings you something that you'd rather not experience, or it hurts another person?

Dear one, first of all, remember that there are no wrong choices. Feel this, own this, take this into your spiritual library and make it part of your life. There are no wrong choices for the divine human. There are only different experiences!

So what are you making a choice about? Are you worried that you are trying to make a decision based upon an energy that is not yours at all? That you might be telepathically or empathically picking up the confusion of another and trying to live their life? For these things are all possible with these times. There are very many other beings now somewhat broadcasting their energies through the ethers and the divine human quite easily picks these up as their own.

So how do you discern what is truly yours and let go of everything that is not? This is a grand question, is it not? And the answer, quite simple actually, is so rarely utilized and yet, is always available to you!

To discern and discover and recognize what is truly your own energy and what is being brought into your energetic field by another, is found through two specific experiences. First of all, when you stop whatever you're doing and experiencing in that moment and simply breathe deeply for a moment, you are bringing your awarenesses and focus back to you, back to your own body. You are bringing that spiritual, intuitive being that you are back into your own body and feeling your own energies.

This being in touch once more with your own body brings you

back to your own awareness. It helps you to feel what is yours in that moment. It helps you to be aware of your experience in that moment and from this home base, so to speak, you can then begin to ask your own intuitive self what you would like to know.

The answers that you receive when you are fully present in your own body, are more likely to be based upon what is occurring in your life, brought to you by your own guides and knowing, than if you were trying to figure things out while being outside of yourself.

The next manner of connecting with yourself to truly discern what is your energy and what is not, is via the time out, the meditation of sorts. You need not know how to meditate nor even to try to meditate. It is in the process of quieting yourself, of taking yourself off for a time, a walk in the park or sitting quietly in a room with the door closed. It is these times that you provide the setting and the opportunity for your own soul self and guides to come to you and bring you knowing, perceiving and potentials for what you are struggling with at any time.

To receive answers and direction, it is most important that you provide the opportunity for your self to communicate with you! Many times there are so many energies swirling around you that the small, knowing voice of your own self is lost in the crowd. And when you give yourself the opportunity to be hear in the quiet of your own surroundings, then you will know that which is your own voice and that which does not belong to you.

I AM Zaihada and I bring you much love and compassion and many blessings from those who work so closely with you on the other side of the veil. You are supported by all of Creation and greatly honored and revered for all that you have chosen in your life. Trust yourself in your choices and let go of that which does not serve the divine human
master that you are!

If today is your birthday: This is a wondrous day, a special day for you. Take the time to celebrate yourself and do something that truly serves you. Gift yourself with time from others, or gift yourself with time that is not wearisome or burdensome but is fun for you! This is your day to shine and so it is.

You Will Know

I greet you this day dear one!

I AM Adamus St. Germaine and I am delighted to come forward this day, in this divine moment, to share this energy with you now. You have come to a place of beingness within the human body where this information can now be received with ease and enjoyment and perhaps with some easing of spirit as well.

Your brain, your mind is weary. Your brain has been overtaxed and overexerted for eons of lives which are contained within the energetic patterns of your DNA. Your mind takes on the patterns of every ancestor you've ever had and it is doing it's best to sort through all those filing cabinets of experiences and learnings in every moment to try and help figure out what it is that you, the divine human, is creating.

And dear one, it is weary beyond imagining with this job! And I say to you this day, at this moment, that the job of trying to figure anything out, to be the problem solver or the troubleshooter is a job that your brain, your mind, has had enough of in this lifetime. It is time to fire your mind from this job and move on.

I ask that you take a moment and breathe deeply of the energies that are present in this moment. You have come to a place of vibrational patterning that you are now able to perceive the next part of this message. And that is about your own knowing, the knowing of the divine human that is always there for you, regardless of the situation, regardless of the circumstances, regardless of what you may or may not believe of yourself.

Take a moment now and simply be at peace and breathe deeply. This breathing brings the human awareness back to the body and it brings a quieting of energies as the body aligns in the breath with the spirit. It is within this place, this now moment, that you will have available to you in very moment, everything that you need to KNOW in that moment.

Say you are struggling with what to do about your job. Take yourself off and be quiet. Breathe with yourself. Find that center that is you connecting with your soul essence, that place where all of you comes together in peacefulness and ease. And within that safe and sacred space, simply ask your divine guidance, that soul self that knows everything that you will ever need to know, what would be the most appropriate choice for you to make.

And then listen! Listen to the small voice that is present with you. Listen with your heart and let go of trying to figure out what you are receiving with your brain, for it will not be able to bring you the best solution for you in that moment. For your brain is linear. And in the New Energy you are no longer functioning in a linear energy! Your poor brain is trying to figure out something that is now being brought into your existence from many other dimensions and realms and it can not handle that!

Now, more than at any other time previous, it is time to trust your knowing. For in every moment you will have the knowing that is exactly what you need, in that moment. Do not try to figure out the future, for it hasn't been created yet. Do not try to figure out what the response of another being will be from your choice, for that is not your problem. The only thing that matters in that moment is what you receive for you.

Trust this, come to rely upon this, and it will get stronger and stronger with use. It is always there for you and will always be there for you. Can you give yourself permission to begin to use it and let your poor brain go back to running your body, which it was always intended to do?

I AM Adamus St. Germaine and I love these times with you! This New Energy is about stepping into the joy and wonder of the evolving and empowered human being and you are truly on your way!

If today is your birthday: What a grand and glorious day it is to begin to trust yourself fully and to cease second guessing what you know is truth for you. Be at peace and enjoy the special love that flows to you on this day. Know that you are dearly loved and never alone.

Release What Isn't Yours to Carry

I AM Raphael, Angel of Healing and Transformation and I greet you in this moment.

You come here to receive these gifts from Heaven, so to speak, and they are delivered to you with great love and joy. It is an grand way to open the door between the realms to receive what is your divine birthright and this time is beloved by all who love you as well.

As a higher consciousness being you have been through the ascension spiral many times, each time going higher and higher as you experience more and more of your own soul's evolution. Each curve of the spiral brings you new experiences, new joys and even new heartaches when you are in the body. And it is in the physical body where the greatest evolutions are able to take place. The physical body is the grand expression of the soul and is the greatest university that exists in all creation. So when you feel those times of wanting to leave the body and be somewhere, even anywhere else, remember that you have a front row seat to the greatest show in all of creation right now.

And as we speak of those experiences that you have in the physical body, I say to you now that you've been carrying far too much energy that does not belong to your body! From almost your first breath upon being birthed into this life you have been the grand empathic being who, out of the greatest love imaginable, takes on the energetic burdens from the shoulders of everyone around you. This is a vastly admirable gift that you offer, yet it now time to put down those burdens and step back.

Each being that is incarnated on this earth comes here with their own path to walk. Yes, you are part of the group of higher consciousness beings who came to this earth to help humanity raise it's level of consciousness and awareness, yet you can no longer do this by taking on the spiritual experiences of another. It is time for each person that you encounter in your life, each person that you've ever known in this lifetime, to take back their own burdens and walk
their own walk.

Take a deep breath dear one, and give yourself permission to put down the many energetic burdens that you've been carrying for those that you love so very much. Give the greatest gift of all to these dear ones, that of supporting them on their own walk, their own path. For when you step to the side of the road and simply observe and cheer them on, this is a far greater gift of love than you could ever give by taking on their burdens.

I AM Raphael and I so love to come here in this way, to take a moment with you during your busy day. To step into your energy and share my love with you. Coming to this place to receive these messages is a grand gift that you give yourself and you are so very worthy of everything that you receive!

If today is your birthday: Today is a day to honor yourself, to celebrate yourself and all that you are. You have a day that belongs only to you and what you do this day is to be celebrated as the expression of you. Know that all the heavens will celebrate with you when you celebrate the wonder that is you.

Keep It Simple

I AM Adamus St. Germaine and I pop in here at this time to share some energies that are a bit of a reminder to many of you. My reputation is that of kicking some behind when necessary, yet at this time I bring in a bit of a softer energy. So relax and allow yourself to be less wary of what I am sharing with you this day!

As the many old energies begin to break up and break down, there will much chaos and confusion with those around you. It is very easy for those of a higher vibration to go into those energies and at times even get lost because you are so open and empathic, always aware of what is around you at all times. Now more than at any other time, taking care of you is something that should come first for you.

You have already done the work that the rest of the world is now coming into experiencing for themselves. Do you need to go through this all again in your life? Oh, there will be times when you do re-experience all these old energies breaking up because you are so easily empathic in your feeling of what others are experiencing. Yet remember that you now are able to move out of what you are feeling from others. Remember to do so and you will be able to retain a measure of peace and balance in your life. Remember "I AM THAT I AM" to find your way back to you.

As these times accelerate and seem to take on a life of their own, keeping things simple in your life will be of great value to you. Others say that they are indeed choosing easy but it doesn't seem to be happening. So what is your definition of easy? Is it seeing a path that magically appears before you without any thought or agenda? So be it. Is it having your life flow without having to make many choices about what to do or not to do? So be it.

And yes, it has been given previously that the true "EASY" path is the one of least resistance. This is a grand delineation and I hope that you allow yourself to live in that energy. What this means dear one, is that if you are experiencing any resistance whatsoever, then it is time to step back and take another look at what is happening.

To often the human tends to over think something, making it more difficult than it needs to be. For in the higher realms, all of existence is easy, flowing with grace and beauty from one moment to another. This is what life on earth is intended to be.

Keep it simple dear human. And when it feels like your life is NOT simple, then give yourself permission to step back and see where you are creating your roadblocks, putting up barriers along the way that slow you down or make you take a new turn. Are you listening to your inner guidance or are you listening to what another is trying to tell you about your life and what you should or shouldn't do?

Above all, give yourself permission to flow with your life as it is.

You have finished with the hard stuff my friend. You have gone through the trials by fire and have walked the desert miles in your bare feet. You have unified with your own divine soul self, your aspects and walk a new path and your inner self knows the way to go in every moment! Can you finally trust yourself enough to let go? Take a deep breath with me now and give yourself a chance.

Now it's time to enjoy all that you've earned and this begins with that life that flows easily for you. Cease creating the difficulties, the suffering and simply BE in every moment, trusting yourself to provide what you need in every moment, every situation. And as you step out of creating a difficult life, you will more and more see how your life can be flowing and easy. And as you do this, you will be bringing to yourself those memories, those reminders of Home, to be here with you now on earth. The more you trust that you already know how to live the simple life, the easier the path.

I AM Adamus and it's always interesting to come and sit with you and share some thoughts, share some energies, and see what comes to reveal itself. Keep your life simple dear friend, for it is and always shall be.

If today is your birthday: Ah, what a perfect day to flow in simple ways. What do you most desire for yourself today? Let go of thinking too much about anything and simply flow with the day as it reveals itself to you in every moment. Follow every impulse and nudging and above all, receive the blessings and love that especially flow to you this day!

Use the Tools

I AM Sophia, Goddess of the Divine Feminine and it is a pleasure to be here with you now.

I am always in the neighborhood, so to speak, yet it is only when I am called forth that I am able to come close to you, to sit and share my energies as I do at this time. Those moments are special and I enjoy them so very much!

Dear one, you have been going through some tough and uncomfortable times and you have felt overwhelmed with your life and what is and isn't happening around you. You have felt a loss of hope and ambition, motivation and direction and over all, have been wondering what in this world you are doing here. I know this dear one, for your energies are clearly visible for all of us here, on this side of the veil, to see and to wonder at for ourselves.

We wonder at all that you are going through dear one, because you have the knowing, and the abilities, to make your life much easier on yourself than you are allowing it to be. We see that you sometimes take the more difficult path along the way when the easier one is quite visible in front of you! We see that you do not so much believe that it's ok now to have the easier life, because the old, not so fun life is all that you have known.

Dear one, you have read an exhausting number of books and channels, have taken in more knowledge that one head can hold at times. You have worked with the energies and you've listened to the masters who bring forth what is available to share. You have walked the walk and talked the talk and still you take the difficult path!

Dear one, I say to you on this day, in this energy of divine love and compassion, that it's time to use the tools that you have already in your tool box, so to speak. You know how to step out of the flow of energies that are all around you of chaos and disharmony. You know how to breathe deeply into yourself to find your center and your own peace of mind. You know exactly what you should or shouldn't do in every moment and can you now simply give yourself permission to have that easier life?

Use the tools that you already have instead of searching for that latest and best "fix" that you feel is out there, waiting to be discovered. Acknowledge that you already know what you need to know to live a grand life. Give yourself permission to use the tools that you already have that will make your life so much easier for you! You've done the hard work, now it's time to enjoy the fruits of those intense labors and be easy on yourself. Use the tools dear one, give yourself permission to be the divine human that you already are now.

I AM Sophia and it's a good day to breathe deeply of what you already know and to acknowledge that you do have what you need in every moment in your life. See within for the solutions and the actions and know that you can fully trust yourself, love yourself, and take care of yourself in every way.

Breathe deeply of the love and compassion that are flowing to you in this moment. Be the divine human and use the tools that you already have... "I AM THAT I AM."

If today is your birthday: What better day is there than this one to step into your knowing that you are already whole, that there is nothing that you need to fix in any way, that you have the foundation within yourself to live the life that you choose. Honor and love yourself this day dear one, for you are loved and blessed beyond imagining!

Choose Your Battle

I greet you this day dear one, with much pleasure that I am able to come in this energy to be with you at this time. There is so very much occurring all around now and having those times to simply take a moment and breathe are not so easy to find!

I AM Adamus St. Germaine and I come to you this day to bring you a simple reminder. Nothing large or earth shaking, yet important none the less as you are moving more and more into those times when you are feeling energies coming at from one side and the other. These energies of ping and pong, right and left, can leave you feeling unbalanced and most definitely frustrated and out of sorts.

Take a moment and simply breathe with me. I bring with me in these moments the opening for many other energies to come and be present with you as well. Give yourself the opportunity to be present with these many energies of love and compassion and image that you are able to take a breath of fresh air in the midst of the chaos that you might be feeling.

What is more and important now dear one, is that you are discerning of where you put your attention and how you put your attention. There are those energies that are now reacting out of their own fear and are looking around to find someone to hold onto and grasp onto rather than deal with their own unbalance.

Much of the fear that is becoming prevalent in this world is from those who are afraid of change, of having their small piece of reality altered in any way. They are comfortable with how things are and would like to see things continue in a like vein rather than go through the uncertainty of change.

And then there are those who find that they are so uncomfortable with the varied energies around them that they are simply going into a place of reacting or acting out as a means of moving uncomfortable energies away from them. They are so greatly uncomfortable that they will use any means of getting rid of this uncertain energy and this may take the form of anger or aggression as the energy moves from them.

Those who are choosing to move their own energies with the expression of negativity want to pull those of a higher vibration into their reality so as to feel less alone. They want someone to save them or to fix them, believing that they themselves do not hold the power nor the ability to sail through any changes or to evolve through any fear.

These ones dear friend, may tug and pull at you and do everything possible to gain your assistance, your attention, and your energy. This is where the discernment comes into play. When you find yourself in such a situation, and especially one where you are yourself feeling greatly uncomfortable overall, this is the time to simply stop and step back for a moment.

This is the moment to stop and ask yourself if this is YOUR problem to deal with. This is the moment to ask yourself if this is YOUR battle to wage. And this is moment to stop and ask yourself if you really feel guided to play a role in whatever scenario is being acted out in that moment.

Dear one, choose your battles. You have the knowing to decide for yourself what you desire to experience and what you would far prefer to step behind the short wall and simply observe. You are not obligated to anyone to participate in their trauma and drama and there is no one who is going to make you do something that you truly do not desire to do... unless that person is you, yourself.

Choose your battles dear one. Choose for yourself what you will or will not play with, what you will or will not participate in with another being. Choose for yourself where you will share your energy and how it will be shared. You do not owe another being anything of yourself and when you stand firm in your knowing of this, it actually brings about an extra energy for another to see that it's possible to make another choice rather than resisting and reacting.

I AM Adamus and it is always a pleasure to come to you in this way and share a moment with you. Remember that you are the creator of your own reality and there is no one who can make you do what you do not truly choose for yourself. Honor your choices and stand firm in your own energy and knowing of what serves you rather than another. It all begins with you my friend.

And in those moments of indecision and stress, remember that the breathing is your first and greatest way to return to yourself and your own knowing!

If today is your birthday: Ah dear one, what will you create for yourself this day? What will you allow for yourself to receive this day of all days? What magic will you allow? What love will you allow to flow to you? For you are deserving of all that is possible for yourself to experience and all your choices to be met. What will you choose for yourself this day of all days? Begin with love my friend, and all else will flow from there!

Surrender

I greet you this day dear one, with much pleasure and delight. For your presence is always one that is much enjoyed by those on this side of the veil and every opportunity that is given when one might come forward to sit with you is lovely indeed.

I AM Sophia, Goddess of the Divine Feminine and I am here this day to remind you of something quite fundamental that brings much ease to the day to day activity of living during these momentous times. I come forward this day to remind you to simply surrender to yourself and to your life that is ever with you and in doing so, you will be in trust and integrity with yourself.

Much of the 4D existence thus far has been about polarity, about resisting and reacting to the myriad energies around you, questioning and sifting through all that is presented to you. It has been about judging and releasing and clearing all that does not align with your own energies.

And now, in this moment, your life becomes more about ease and joy and living in surrender to that which is brought to you now by your own soul self. Are you ready to fully step into living in full and complete trust of your own self? For that is where surrendering comes into play dear one!

Surrender does not in any way mean giving up or giving over, especially not to the energies of another. Surrender is about trusting that everything in your life is in true and total alignment with your path. Surrender is about the knowing that you are always safe, always will be safe, and that there is a higher power and connection that is always present with you. And with that kind of teamwork happening, how can your life be anything less than easy!

As was spoken by our dear friend Tobias many years ago, you can now live your life by creating in broad strokes on your canvas. It is time to let go of the day to day worry about the little details, for those will automatically be taken care of for you. All that is needed by you in your life will be there for at the moment you need it. In every moment, in every now moment, you will have everything that you require.

Surrender to the knowing that the healing is done, the releasing is finished and complete and you are now moving into total and complete unity and balance with your soul self. Surrender to the knowing that this integration and unification brings to you all that you will ever need in your life and all is taken care of in each moment. Surrender to those outer experiences that have in the past brought you into a place of resistance and allow those energies that used to trigger you in a response simply flow on by you.

Those times of lessons are finished as well. Surrender to the flowing of your life now that is free of snags and roadblocks and be at peace dear one, for all is well with your soul. Surrender in every moment to what is being presented to you, experienced by you, in the knowing that it is brought to you by your own higher soul self. Surrender to the knowing that you can be your divine self in every moment.

I AM Sophia and I so love to sit with you and share our energies. Breathe deeply with me for a moment and share the love and compassion that are here for you as well. For many come to sit by the sidelines when a visit with you is involved. Feel their love and feel the support that is available for you, always.

If today is your birthday: You are beloved beyond measure dear one. Never for a moment forget this! And on this special day, remember to allow yourself to receive the many energetic gifts that life has to bring to you as well as the physical gifts that come on this day. Receive the love, receive the compassion and receive the knowing that all is indeed well with your soul!

Express Without Limitation

I greet you this day dear one, in this safe and sacred space, and I dance with your energies as they flow easily between those who are here with you now and the many aspects who read this sharing.

I AM Sophia, Goddess of the Divine Feminine and it is a grand day indeed to be here sharing this energy with you! Being open to the sharing and allowing yourself to receive as you breathe in this energy is a great gift that you can give to yourself. For there is so much love that can flow to you in moments such as this and dear one, this is indeed one of those moments out of time when you can feel the energies of Home come close to you!

It is good, is it not, to take a moment here and there out of your hectic and sometimes wildly spinning day to simply stop and breathe for a moment. This time is yours dear one and it will be what you need it to be each time you come here to read this message, each time it appears before you on the screen. It is here for you and it is a gift that you are giving to yourself.

Much is shifting in this world and at times it can appear as though nothing makes any sense. Forms and structures are being torn down, rules are broken and many, many lies are being revealed so that the truth can then come in once more. This is a grand time dear one, although at times you may not feel so easy about what is all around you.

Yet this is a time now for you to truly express the greatness of who you are! To step into the shoes of the Master and show the world that you are one who has done the work, walked the talk and are fearless in your expression in your life. Now is the time dear one, to express whatever your creations might be and do so without any agenda or limitation! Now is the time to turn loose your creator abilities and paint with those broad strokes. Then stand back and watch your dreams come true.

You've kept yourself apart for much of this journey as being with others has at times been painful and heartbreaking for you. There have been those many times when those around you did not understand you in the least and you felt like an alien in human form! Well dear one, you are!!! You are an angel in human form and it's now time to step up and shine that divine light and begin to show the world who you really are.

Express your divinity without limitation and allow your creations to take on their own life and come to their fullest evolution without trying to control any of it. Being the divine creator means painting with those broad strokes and then the creations themselves take on a new life and begin to fill in the details without any effort from you whatsoever. It is time now to flow your creations and also to flow your life, for the expression of your life works in much the same way.

Express your life without limitation and without agenda or definition of how this or that must or should be. The times for coloring within the lines are long past you now dear one, for the pages of your coloring book will shift and flow under your crayons as you color and will become grand rainbows and kaleidoscopes of creations as you gave at them. All energies will shift with you in your creations and when you are in allowance of this and know that whatever comes from your creations will be in perfect form and function, then you can sit back and enjoy the view!

I AM Sophia and it is a delight to be here with you this day. So much is changing and at times you have your doubts about your path. Breathe with all who are here with you in this moment and know that all is well with your soul. You are doing just fine.

If today is your birthday: Go out this day and celebrate the grandness of who you are! Share your energies with others and see how their eyes light up as they move through their own struggles and confusion. See the way they reflect back to you the wonder of who you are and then have some cake and ice cream and some fun!! You are so dearly loved!!

Believe in You

I am with you this day beloved one and I am always with you in spirit. I AM the collective voice of those many angelic beings who are your own team, your own support staff so to speak. The ones who hold you close when you feel alone and unloved. The ones who cheer you on during those moments of personal triumph and success. We are always with you dearest one because we are a team!

I speak to you this day about taking care of you and most importantly, believing in yourself. For with the times being what they are it is not so easy to find yourself at times. To hold onto that vision and that energy that is uniquely yours and to trust in what you are perceiving in every moment.

For those energies of dis-trust are rampant and chaos of spirit and being is the goal in this type of fearful energy. There are many who have great fear about those grand beings who stand in their own power and follow their own guidance rather than what they are told to do. And the more that you are able to trust yourself in every moment, with every choice and scenario that is presented to you, the stronger in self you become.

Believing in yourself is paramount right now dearest one. For you are your dearest friend now more than at any other time. It is your heart that knows the way and your mind that carries the interpretations and analyses of what comes to you. It is not some voice on the television or what you are reading in the newspaper, for they do not know you. No one knows you the way that you know yourself and therefore no one can ever make fully considered decisions of any kind for you because they don't know YOU!

Believe in you now dearest one, for you have the answers that you seek, always. Believe in you when you are troubled, for you have a divine soul that is always with you and guides your every step when you get out of the way! Much of what comes to you in the form of voices or uncomfortable energies are not yours and they do not have your best interests at hand. It is only your own soul that is fully behind you and every decision that you will make in this life. Is that not something worthy of trust?

Believe in you that you will make those decisions that are in alignment with your divine being and in harmony with what is written in your soul chart. Believe in you and release the illusions of self-doubt that have been a fun experience to have and now have far outlived their usefulness. For doubt is not an energy that needs to be in your life anymore dearest one. Haven't you had more than enough of the experiencing of what it's like to doubt your every move?

Believe in yourself now beloved one and know that you are making those decisions and choices that fully support you and your path, even when you wonder if this is true for you. For you are a grand divine human and there are no wrong choices. Every choice serves you in every way and it also serves those around you in ways that you may never see in this life. Yet when you return to us on this side of the veil you will see that you walk in divine light and are loved indeed for all that you do.

Believe in you now dearest one and be at peace. For all is well with your soul and it is time to live the life that you deserve. Let go of whatever roadblocks and burdens you carry that tell you differently, for they too have long since outlived their own purpose. Listen to your own voice and follow your heart beloved one. And live in joy, always.

If today is your birthday: Today is a perfect day to begin to live in your heart and to follow what is shares with you. Take yourself apart from the day to day world and listen for that voice that brings you the knowing of how to proceed in every moment. Be open to the love that flows so strongly to you now and be patient with yourself, releasing the doubt. Know that you are so dearly loved this day and all days and hold your head high in every moment. You are a divine human and all is well.

BREATHE!!

About the Facilitator

Jeane R. Pothier has been doing channeled messages from Spirit for over eleven years now via email, chat rooms and the Internet. Her background includes years of in-depth research into metaphysics, alternative medicine, Shamanism and spiritualism while seeking insight to her own personal experiences and answers to questions about these shifting times. The clarity of her energies are foundational for the messages that come through from the other realms, as they are transmitted without editing and changes, bringing through the great love and compassion available to all from those beloved ones beyond the veil.

To read other channels, please visit www.answers-and-more.com

www.ingramcontent.com/pod-product-compliance
Lightning Source LLC
Chambersburg PA
CBHW031331040426
42443CB00005B/300